THE PROSPEROUS PEN

Mastering Freelance Writing for Retirement Riches

ROBERT J BANNON

Dedication

Dedicated to all the lifelong learners who live by the motto,

"It's never too late."

Contents

INTRODUCTION

Ah, the whimsical world of freelance writing—a realm where creativity dances with deadlines, and the only boss you answer to is your muse (and the occasional cup of coffee). If you've ever found yourself daydreaming about crafting sentences in your pajamas or turning your love for words into a paycheck, then you, my friend, are standing at the vibrant intersection of passion and profession.

In this comprehensive journey through the craft of freelancing, we'll navigate the twists and turns of a writer's imagination, unraveling the mysteries of client emails, the sacred bond between a writer and their favorite thesaurus, and the delicate art of balancing productivity with the allure of cat videos on the internet.

So, grab your favorite pen (or keyboard), settle into your coziest writing nook, and prepare to embark on a literary adventure, where every word is a brushstroke on the canvas of your freelance dreams. Let the tales of typos, triumphs, and the occasional bout of writer's block unfold in this detailed exploration of the writer's life. Welcome to the enchanting world where commas have personalities, deadlines have a sense of humor, and every page is a new chapter in the wonderful world of freelance writing!

But first, let's review the 5 simple income generators for retired people with limited online marketing knowledge that we outlined in book 1 of this series, *EXTRA RETIREMENT INCOME IS SEXY*.

1. **Freelance Writing:** Many websites and businesses constantly need content. If you enjoy writing, you could offer your services as a freelance writer. There are platforms like Upwork and Fiverr that connect writers with clients. We will explore this opportunity in depth in this book.

2. **Online Tutoring:** If you have expertise in a particular subject, you could offer online tutoring services. Platforms like Chegg Tutors or Wyzant allow you to connect with students seeking help. More information about online

tutoring is available in book 3 of this series, ***DIGITAL CLASSROOMS.***

3. **Virtual Assistance:** Many entrepreneurs and small businesses need help with tasks like email management, data entry, and scheduling. There are many job search sources like Fiverr, Upwork and TaskRabbit. Offering virtual assistance services can be a great way to use your organizational skills. We will dive into becoming a virtual assistant in book 4, ***SILVER HAIRED SAGE.***

4. **Sell Handmade Crafts or Digital Items:** If you have a talent for crafting or have accumulated unique vintage items, you can sell them on platforms like Etsy or eBay. Creating digital products like ebooks, courses and journals can lead to a world of opportunity. This exciting area of income generation is fully explained in book 5 of this series, ***DESIGNING WEALTH***.

5. **Take part in Online Surveys and Reviews:** While it may not generate a substantial sum of money, participating in online surveys can

provide a small stream of income. Websites like Swagbucks or Survey Junkie offer opportunities to earn money for your opinions. Creating and sharing product reviews can lead to a very substantial income generating business. We offer all the details of this business idea in book 6, ***GOLDEN INSIGHTS***.

Remember, the key is to find something you enjoy and are comfortable doing. In this text, we will focus on the incredible world of FREELANCE WRITING. You can find our books on the other areas of retiree income where you bought this one.

FORWARD

Welcome to the rewarding world of **"THE PROSPEROUS PEN: Mastering Freelance Writing for Retirement Riches"** – the guide that turns your way with words into a golden ticket to financial freedom! Whether you are struggling with not enough income in retirement or are just tired of watching daytime TV, you're in for a treat.

"THE PROSPEROUS PEN: Mastering Freelance Writing for Retirement Riches" – is a journey of inspiration, empowerment, and the boundless possibilities that come with wielding the power of words. If you've ever dared to dream of a retirement filled with both financial abundance and creative fulfillment, you're in the right place.

This book is more than just a guide; it's a friendly companion on your quest to transform your passion for writing into a lucrative and fulfilling freelance career. Picture yourself not just writing words but crafting a lifestyle where every sentence brings you closer to the retirement you've envisioned.

As we embark on this journey, we'll reveal the world of freelance writing with a focus on encouragement and practical advice. You'll discover the joy of turning your creativity into a source of income and learn how to navigate the exciting landscape of freelancing with confidence.

So, whether you're a seasoned wordsmith or just starting to pen your dreams, "**THE PROSPEROUS PEN**" is here to cheer you on. Your retirement dreams are within reach, and this book is your guide to unlocking the door to a future where your words not only tell stories but also build the foundation for the retirement you deserve. Get ready to be inspired, empowered, and embark on a journey where your pen becomes the key to your prosperity. Let's turn your writing aspirations into a roadmap for a rich and fulfilling retirement.

Chapter 1

FREELANCE WRITING

Freelance writing can be a very enjoyable and profitable part time (or full time) endeavor and the need continues to grow year after year. There are some things that we need to know and do in order to be successful.

- **Identify Your Niche:**

Determine what topics or industries you are knowledgeable about or passionate about. This could be anything from technology and finance to health, travel, or lifestyle.

- **Create a Portfolio:**

Develop a portfolio that showcases your writing skills. Include samples of your work, even if they are pieces you've written for personal projects.

This portfolio will be crucial for attracting potential clients.

- **Set Up Profiles on Freelance Platforms:**

Sign up on freelance platforms like Upwork, Fiverr, or Freelancer. Create a compelling profile that highlights your skills, experience, and the type of writing services you offer.

- **Bid on Projects:**

Browse through the writing projects on these platforms and submit proposals to the ones that match your expertise. Tailor your proposals for each job, showcasing your understanding of the client's needs.

- **Build Relationships:**

Once you start getting projects, focus on building positive relationships with your clients. Deliver high-quality work on time and communicate effectively to ensure client satisfaction.

- **Network:**

Join online writing communities or forums where clients and writers interact. Networking can lead to direct opportunities and help you stay informed about potential writing gigs.

- **Set Your Rates:**

Determine your pricing structure. Consider factors such as the complexity of the project, the time required, and your level of expertise. Be competitive, but also value your time and skills. A good rule of thumb to remember is that clients are not just paying you for the hour you spent writing but the lifetime you spent learning how to do it.

- **Expand Your Skills:**

As you gain more experience, consider expanding your skill set. This could include learning about SEO writing, content marketing, or other specialized areas that are in demand.

- **Market Yourself.**

Use social media and other online platforms to market your freelance writing services. Share your portfolio, engage with potential clients, and showcase your expertise through blog posts or articles. Add a line about your freelance writing to your email signature line.

Remember, building a freelance writing career takes time and persistence. It's about establishing a reputation for delivering quality work and building a network of satisfied clients.

Chapter 2

WHAT IS FREELANCE WRITING

Let's delve deeper into the world of freelance writing:

- **Content Types:**

Freelance writing isn't just limited to articles. You can explore various types of content, including blog posts, website copy, product descriptions, social media content, whitepapers, eBooks, and more. Diversifying your skill set can open up a range of opportunities.

- **Pitching to Magazines and Publications:**

Beyond online platforms, consider pitching your writing to magazines and online publications. Research magazines or websites that align with your interests and expertise and send them tailored pitches for articles.

- **Guest Blogging:**

Offer to write guest posts for blogs within your niche. This not only provides exposure, but also allows you to include these pieces in your portfolio. Many blogs accept guest contributions and often provide a byline with a link back to your profile.

- **Building a Personal Blog:**

Start your own blog to showcase your writing style and expertise. This can serve as a central hub for potential clients to learn more about you. Consistently updating your blog with relevant and valuable content can also attract organic traffic.

- **Content Mills vs. Private Clients:**

Content mills are platforms where you can find a high volume of writing jobs, but they often pay less. As you gain experience, try to transition towards acquiring private clients. Building relationships with businesses or individuals directly can lead to more stable and higher-paying gigs.

- **Developing a Writing Specialty:**

If you have a particular interest or expertise, consider specializing in a niche. Clients often prefer writers who understand their industry, and this specialization can set you apart from generalist writers.

- **Professionalism and Communication:**

Being a successful freelance writer isn't just about writing well; it's also about professionalism and effective communication. Respond to messages promptly, meet deadlines, and be open to feedback. A positive and professional attitude can lead to repeat business and referrals.

- **Learning Basic SEO:**

Understanding the basics of Search Engine Optimization (SEO) can make your writing more appealing to clients. Many businesses seek writers who can create content that not only engages readers but also ranks well in search engine results.

- **Continuous Learning.**

The writing landscape is constantly evolving. Stay updated on industry trends, new writing techniques, and changes in search engine algorithms. Continuous learning will keep your skills sharp and make you more marketable.

Freelance writing is not just a job; it's a business. Treat your writing career with a high level of profes- sionalism and dedication, and you'll find it to be a rewarding and flexible way to generate income.

Chapter 3

IDENTIFY A NICHE

Identifying your niche is a crucial step in establishing a successful freelance writing career. Your niche is the specific subject or industry you specialize in. Here are some steps to help you identify and define your niche:

1. **Self-Reflection:**

   - **Interests:** Consider your personal interests and passions. Writing about topics you genuinely enjoy will not only make your work more enjoyable but will also likely result in higher quality writing.

   - **Expertise:** Assess your professional and personal expertise. What knowledge or skills do you possess that others might find valuable? Your background or career history can be a significant starting point for finding your niche.

2. **Research Market Demand:**

- ◦ **Identify Trends:** Research current trends and topics in the writing market. Look for subjects that are in demand but not over-saturated with writers. Emerging trends or specialized areas can present unique opportunities.

- ◦ **Analyze Competitors:** Study other free-lance writers in your chosen platforms or niche. Understand what topics they focus on and identify gaps or areas where you can provide a unique perspective.

- ◦ **Where to Look:** Spend time on the various sites like Fiverr, Upwork and others looking at what writers offer and what buyers are asking for. This will help you find niches and compatible job opportunities.

3. **Consider Audience Needs:**

- ◦ **Who is Your Ideal Reader:** Define

your target audience. Understanding who you're writing for can help you tailor your content to meet their needs and preferences.

- **Problem-Solving:** Consider how your writing can solve problems or provide valuable information to your audience. Identifying the needs of your target market will guide your niche selection.

4. **Evaluate Your Unique Voice:**

- **Personal Style:** Reflect on your personal writing style. What tone, voice, or style do you naturally gravitate towards? Your unique voice can be a defining factor in attracting clients who resonate with your writing style. This could incorporate everything including persuasive, technical, academic, humorous and even poetry. What do you want to do?

5. **Test and Refine:**

- **Experiment:** In the early stages, don't be

afraid to experiment with different topics or industries. Write a variety of articles or blog posts to see what you enjoy the most and where your strengths lie.

◦ **Feedback:** Pay attention to feedback from clients and readers. Positive feedback can show that you're on the right track, while constructive criticism can help you refine your skills and niche.

6. **Combine Interests and Market Demand:**

◦ **Overlap:** Look for areas where your personal interests overlap with market demand. Combining your passions with what clients are looking for can create a niche that is both fulfilling and profitable.

7. **Stay Flexible.**

◦ **Adapt to Changes:** The writing market evolves, and so should your niche. Stay open to adjusting your focus based on emerging trends, changes in your interests, or shifts in market demand.

Remember that finding the right niche may take time, and it's okay to adjust your focus as you gain more experience and learn more about what resonates with both you and your audience. Your niche should be a balance between what you love to write about and what potential clients are seeking.

Self editing your work is essential but if you feel challenged in that area then using an app like ProWritingAid is the best solution. Go to their website and look. It is a small investment in helping you become a professional writer.

Chapter 4

WRITING PORTFOLIO

Creating a strong online writing portfolio is essential for showcasing your skills and attracting potential clients as a beginner freelance writer. Here are some steps and suggestions to help you build an effective portfolio:

1. **Choose a Platform:**

   - **Personal Website:** Consider creating a personal website using platforms like WordPress, Wix, or Squarespace. Having your own domain name (e.g., yourname.com) adds a professional touch.

   - **Portfolio Platforms:** Use specialized portfolio platforms like Contently, Clippings.me, or Journo Portfolio. These platforms showcase writing samples.

2. **Include a Bio and Contact Information:**

- ◦ **Introduction:** Write a brief bio that introduces yourself, highlighting your writing background, interests, and any relevant expertise, professional accreditation or employment.

- ◦ **Contact Details:** Make it easy for potential clients to get in touch by including your professional email address or a contact form.

3. **Select Your Best Samples:**

- ◦ **Quality Over Quantity:** Choose a selection of your best work rather than including everything. Focus on pieces that show your writing style, versatility, and ability to engage readers.

- ◦ **Diversify Content:** If possible, showcase a variety of writing types, such as blog posts, articles, product descriptions, or any other relevant content.

4. **Provide Context for Each Piece:**

- **Annotations:** Accompany each sample with a short annotation or description. Explain the context of the piece, the target audience, and any positive outcomes or feedback received.

- **Client Testimonials:** If you have received positive feedback from clients, consider including brief testimonials to build credibility. Please check with the person or company and ask permission if you intend to make their name public.

5. **Optimize for Readability:**

- **Formatting:** Present your portfolio in a clean, organized format. Use a consistent font and make sure the layout is easy to navigate.

- **Images:** Include relevant images or graphics to enhance visual appeal. If you wrote content for a specific website, consider including screenshots.

6. **Highlight Your Niche:**

- **Emphasize Specialization:** If you've chosen a niche or have expertise in a particular industry, highlight this in your portfolio. Clients often look for writers who understand their specific needs.

- **Create Sections:** Group your samples into sections based on themes or topics to make it easier for clients to find relevant content.

7. **Update Regularly:**

- **Fresh Content:** Keep your portfolio up to date with your latest and best work. Regularly add new samples to showcase ongoing improvement and versatility.

- **Blog Section:** If you have a blog, include a link for it in your portfolio. This can show your consistency in producing content and your ability to engage an audience.

8. **Share Your Portfolio.**

- **Include Links:** Share the link to your portfolio on your resume, LinkedIn profile, and other professional social media platforms.

○ **Networking:** Actively share your portfolio with potential clients, colleagues, and within relevant online communities. Networking is crucial for getting your work noticed.

By taking the time to curate a professional and well-organized online writing portfolio, you increase your chances of making a positive impression on potential clients and establishing yourself as a competent freelance writer.

Chapter 5

YOUR PROFILE

Creating a successful online profile is essential for freelancers and any professional looking to make a positive impression on potential clients or employers. Almost every area of creating additional income requires a profile and we keep emphasizing it with additional ideas so that you can constantly improve yours. You probably realize that a profile is never finished as we move from project to project and success to success. Always be prepared to change and update it according to your target audience. Here are the key elements to consider when crafting an effective online profile:

1. **Professional Profile Picture:**

   - Use a high-quality, professional-looking headshot.

- Ensure good lighting and a clean background.

- Choose an image that reflects your personality and aligns with your professional image.

2. **Compelling Headline:**

- Craft a headline that succinctly describes your expertise or the value you provide.

- Include keywords relevant to your skills or industry.

3. **Engaging Summary or Bio:**

- Write a concise and engaging summary that highlights your skills, experience, and what sets you apart.

- Showcase your personality while maintaining a professional tone.

- Include information about your professional goals and passions.

4. **Relevant Skills and Endorsements:**

- List key skills that apply to your profession or the services you offer.

- Seek endorsements from colleagues, clients, or other professionals to validate your skills.

5. **Detailed Work Experience:**

- Provide a comprehensive overview of your work experience.

- Focus on achievements and specific contributions in each role.

- Use quantifiable metrics that show their impact.

6. **Education and Certifications:**

- Include details about your educational background, emphasizing degrees, certifications, and relevant coursework.

- Highlight any certifications or professional development that enhance your expertise including non-accredited courses you have completed that are relevant..

7. **Portfolio or Showcase of Work:**

- ○ If applicable, link to a portfolio or showcase of your work.

- ○ Include samples that show the breadth and quality of your skills.

8. **Client Testimonials and Recommendations:**

- ○ Feature positive testimonials or recommendations from clients or colleagues.

- ○ Showcase specific projects or achievements that highlight your strengths.

- ○ It is appropriate to mention commendations that are not connected to your workplace, such as military or citizenship awards.

9. **Contact Information:**

- ○ Provide clear and professional contact information.

- Include your email address or a preferred method of contact.

10. **Customized URL:**

- If possible, create a customized and easily readable URL for your profile.

- This makes it easier for people to find and remember your profile.

11. **Keywords for Search Optimization:**

- Integrate relevant keywords throughout your profile to enhance discoverability.

- Use terms commonly searched for in your industry.

12. **Consistency Across Platforms:**

- Ensure consistency in your professional brand across different platforms.

- Use the same profile picture, headline, and key information on your resume, LinkedIn, personal website, and other professional platforms.

13. **Regular Updates:**

- ○ Keep your profile up to date with the latest information, skills, and achievements.

- ○ Regular updates show your commitment to professional growth.

14. **Engagement:**

- ○ Actively engage with your network by participating in discussions, sharing relevant content, and connecting with professionals in your industry.

Remember that your online profile serves as a digital representation of your professional identity, so investing time and effort into making it interesting and accurate is crucial for success in the online professional landscape.

Chapter 6

BID ON PROJECTS

B idding on projects as a new freelance writer is a competitive process, but there are several keys to increasing your chances of success. Here are some tips for effective bidding:

1. **Understand the Project Requirements:**

   - Carefully read and understand the project description. Make sure you can fulfil the client's needs before placing a bid.

2. **Tailor Your Proposals:**

   - Avoid generic proposals. Tailor each bid to the specific project, addressing the client's needs and requirements.

   - Mention specific details from the project description to show that you've thoroughly read it.

3. **Highlight Relevant Experience:**

   - Emphasize your relevant experience and skills. If you have previous work that aligns with the project, showcase it in your bid.

   - Explain how your background uniquely qualifies you for the job.

4. **Showcase Your Writing Style:**

   - Include a brief sample or link to previous work that showcases your writing style. This helps the client gauge your ability to meet their expectations.

5. **Set Realistic and Competitive Rates:**

   - Research the average rates for similar projects in your niche and location.

   - Set a competitive rate that reflects your skills and experience as a new freelancer.

   - Submitting a bid that is obviously extremely low will be a red flag for potential clients;

give value to your abilities.

6. **Demonstrate Professionalism:**

   ◦ Use a professional and courteous tone in your bids.

   ◦ Showcase your reliability by addressing deadlines and any potential challenges up-front.

7. **Ask Questions:**

   ◦ If there's any ambiguity in the project description, ask clarifying questions. This not only shows your interest, but also helps you submit a more accurate proposal.

8. **Provide a Clear Timeline:**

   ◦ Outline a realistic timeline for completing the project. Clients appreciate freelancers who can deliver quality work within specified deadlines.

9. **Create a Standout Profile:**

   ◦ Develop a comprehensive and well-written freelancer profile that highlights your skills, experience, and writing style.

- ◦ Include a professional profile picture to add a personal touch.

- ◦ See the previous chapter for more information.

10. **Be Responsive:**

- ◦ Respond promptly to client messages and inquiries. Timeliness and responsiveness indicate professionalism and reliability.

11. **Offer Value:**

- ◦ Clearly articulate the value you bring to the project. Explain how your unique skills can contribute to the success of the client's goals.

12. **Start Small and Gain Reviews:**

- ◦ As a new freelancer, consider bidding on smaller projects to build your reputation.

- ◦ Positive client reviews are crucial for gaining trust and attracting more opportunities.

○ Going the extra mile, especially at the beginning, will have a major impact on the quantity and quality of your feedback.

13. **Be Honest About Your Experience:**

○ Be transparent about your level of experience. If you're new to freelancing, emphasize your enthusiasm to learn and your commitment to delivering quality work.

14. **Follow Up.**

○ If you haven't heard from a client after submitting a bid, consider sending a polite follow-up message to express your continued interest.

Remember, persistence is key. It may take time to secure your first few projects, but as you build a positive track record and gain more experience, you'll likely find more success in winning bids.

Chapter 7

BUILD RELATIONSHIPS

Building strong relationships is essential for success in any freelance business, including freelance writing. Here are some effective ways to build relationships as you launch your freelance writing business:

1. **Create a Professional Online Presence:**

   ○ Develop a professional and polished online presence. This includes a well-crafted freelancer profile on platforms like Upwork, Fiverr or LinkedIn, as well as a personal website showcasing your portfolio.

2. **Engage in Networking:**

   ○ Actively take part in online forums, social media groups, and communities relevant to your niche. Engage in conversations, share insights, and offer assistance to others in the community.

3. **Attend Industry Events:**

- Attend virtual or in-person events, conferences, and workshops related to writing or your specific niche. These events provide excellent opportunities to connect with fellow writers and potential clients.

4. **Join Freelance Platforms:**

- Join freelance platforms and bid on projects. Building relationships with clients is crucial for securing repeat business and positive referrals.

5. **Offer Value:**

- Provide value to your network by sharing relevant and helpful content. This could include writing tips, industry insights, or sharing interesting articles related to your niche.

6. **Connect with Other Freelancers:**

- ○ Build relationships with other freelancers in your field. They can be valuable sources of advice, collaboration opportunities, and referrals.

7. **Seek Feedback:**

- ○ Request feedback on your work. Constructive criticism not only helps you improve but also shows your commitment to delivering high-quality work.

8. **Follow Up with Clients:**

- ○ After completing a project, follow up with clients to express your gratitude for the opportunity. Inquire about their satisfaction and ask for feedback. This can lead to long-term relationships.

9. **Be Reliable and Professional:**

- ○ Deliver work on time and maintain a high level of professionalism. Reliable and professional behavior builds trust and strengthens relationships with clients.

10. **Personalize Your Interactions:**

- When reaching out to potential clients or collaborators, personalize your messages. Mention specific details about their work or projects to show genuine interest.

11. **Build an Email List:**

- Start an email newsletter or mailing list to stay in touch with clients and prospects. Share updates, new achievements, or relevant content to keep them engaged.

- It is advisable to provide some value in your emails rather than constantly pitching to your prospects.

12. **Offer Incentives:**

- Consider offering incentives for referrals or repeat business. This could include discounts on future projects or additional services at a reduced rate. Creating helpful cheat sheets in your niche and offering them as a bonus would be valuable to your clients.

13. **Collaborate on Projects:**

- Collaborate with other freelancers or businesses on projects. This not only expands your network, but also opens the door to future collaborative opportunities.

14. **Be Active on Social Media:**

- Use social media platforms to connect with potential clients and fellow writers. Share your expertise, engage in conversations, and build relationships organically.

15. **Express Gratitude.**

- Show appreciation for your clients and collaborators. A simple thank-you message can go a long way in building a positive relationship.

Building relationships takes time, so be patient and genuine in your interactions. The goal is to establish a network of connections that can support your freelance writing business over the long term.

Chapter 8

NETWORK

Effective networking can significantly benefit your freelance writing business. Here are some of the best places to network as a freelance writer:

1. **Freelance Platforms:**

   ○ Websites like Upwork, Freelancer, and Fiverr provide platforms for freelancers to connect with clients. Actively take part in these platforms by bidding on projects and engaging with potential clients.

2. **LinkedIn:**

   ○ LinkedIn is a powerful professional networking platform. Create a strong profile, join relevant groups, and connect with professionals in your industry. Share your expertise through posts and articles.

3. **Industry-Specific Forums and Communities:**

   ○ Join online forums and communities related to your writing niche. Websites like Reddit, Quora, or specialized forums in your industry are great places to engage in conversations and build relationships.

4. **Conferences and Workshops:**

   ○ Attend virtual or in-person conferences, workshops, and seminars related to writing, content creation, or your specific niche. These events provide excellent opportunities to connect with industry professionals.

5. **Social Media Groups:**

   ○ Join and actively participate in social media groups relevant to your writing niche. Platforms like Facebook and X/Twitter often have groups where professionals discuss industry trends, share opportunities, and network.

6. **Local Networking Events:**

- Attend local networking events, meetups, or workshops. Check out events hosted by business organizations, writing groups, or chambers of commerce in your area.

7. **Guest Blogging:**

- Contribute guest posts to reputable blogs in your niche. This not only showcases your writing skills but also exposes you to the blog's audience, potential clients, and other writers.

8. **Online Writing Communities:**

- Join online writing communities where writers share tips, resources, and opportunities. Websites like Wattpad, Scribophile, or Absolute Write can be great places to connect with fellow writers.

9. **Content Creation Platforms:**

- Platforms like Medium or Vocal Media allow writers to publish and share their work. Engage with the community, leave thoughtful comments, and connect with writers and readers.

10. **Podcast and Webinar Attendances:**

- Attend webinars and podcasts related to writing or your niche. Many of these events have interactive features that allow you to connect with hosts and other attendees.

11. **Alumni Networks:**

- If you have a college or university background, leverage alumni networks. Alumni events and online platforms can connect you with professionals who share a common educational background.

12. **Collaboration Platforms:**

- Platforms like Collabwrite or Skyword connect writers with businesses looking for content creators. Explore collaboration opportunities that align with your expertise.

13. **Book and Author Events:**

- Attend book launches, author readings, and literary events. These gatherings often attract writers, editors, and other professionals in the writing and publishing industry. Many writers now create virtual launches and discussion groups through sites like Goodreads and others.

14. **Writing Conventions:**

- Take part in writing conventions or book fairs. These events offer networking opportunities with authors, publishers, and other professionals in the writing world.

15. **Online Courses and Workshops.**

- Enrol in online courses related to writing or content creation. These courses often provide discussion forums where you can interact with instructors and fellow students.

Remember to approach networking with authenticity and a willingness to contribute to the community. Building relationships takes time, so focus on creating genuine connections and adding value to the conversation, rather than solely seeking immediate benefits for your freelance writing business.

Chapter 9

SETTING RATES

Setting your freelance writing rates can be challenging as a new writer, but it's crucial to establish rates that reflect your skills, expertise, and the value you bring to clients. Here's a step-by-step guide to help you determine your rates:

1. **Research Industry Standards:**

    ○ Investigate the average rates for freelance writers in your niche and location. This research will provide a baseline for setting competitive yet realistic rates.

2. **Consider Your Expenses:**

    ○ Calculate your living expenses, including rent, utilities, insurance, and other bills. Factor in costs related to your freelance business, such as software subscriptions, the Internet, and any professional development you plan to pursue.

3. **Determine Your Desired Income:**

- Decide on your desired annual income as a freelancer. Consider how many hours you plan to work per week and how many weeks per year you expect to be actively freelancing.

4. **Calculate an Hourly Rate:**

- Divide your desired annual income by the number of billable hours you expect to work in a year. Keep in mind that freelancers often spend non-billable hours on administrative tasks, marketing, and professional development.

$$HourlyRate = DesiredAnnualIncome/(BillableHours + Non-BillableHours)$$

This is a very simplistic formula for determining your hourly rate, but it is a place to start. You will adjust your rates as you get more gigs.

1. **Evaluate Your Skill Level:**

   - Assess your skill level and experience. If you have specialized knowledge or expertise in a particular niche, you may command higher rates.

2. **Consider Market Demand:**

   - Evaluate the demand for your specific writing skills in the market. If your niche is in high demand, you may have more flexibility in setting higher rates.

3. **Start Conservatively:**

   - As a new freelancer, consider starting with a conservative rate that aligns with your skills and experience. You can gradually increase your rates as you gain more expertise and build a strong portfolio.

4. **Factor in Additional Services:**

   - If you offer additional services such as editing, proofreading, or SEO optimization, consider incorporating these into your pricing structure.

5. **Create Different Packages:**

- ○ Offer clients different packages based on the scope of the project. For example, you could have an introductory package for a set number of words, a standard package with additional services, and a premium package for more complex projects.

6. **Communicate Value to Clients:**

- ○ When discussing rates with clients, clearly communicate the value you bring to their projects. Emphasize how your expertise can benefit their business or organization.

7. **Be Flexible but Firm:**

- ○ Be open to negotiation, especially when starting out. However, establish a bottom line that you cannot go below to ensure you are fairly compensated for your work. Being the lowest priced bidder is not always the best approach for a freelancer.

8. **Track Your Time:**

- Use time-tracking tools to monitor the time you spend on different projects. This can help you evaluate whether your rates are reasonable based on the effort involved.

- Some easy to use online time tracking tools include, Clockify, Toggl Track, TopTracker, MyHours and Hours (for Apple users).

- It is good to get used to tracking since you may be working on multiple projects at the same time.

9. **Review and Adjust Regularly.**

- Periodically review your rates and adjust them based on changes in your skills, experience, and the market demand for your services.

Remember that setting your rates is a dynamic process, and it's okay to adjust them as your freelance writing business grows. Regularly reassess your rates to ensure they align with your skills, market demand, and the value you bring to your clients.

Chapter 10

EXPAND YOUR SKILLS

Constantly expanding your skills is crucial for staying relevant and competitive in any field, including freelance writing. Here are some effective ways to enhance your skills as a freelance writer:

Read Widely:

Read a diverse range of materials, including books, articles, and blogs. Exposing yourself to different writing styles, genres, and perspectives can broaden your own writing capabilities.

Many bestselling authors have stated that you cannot be a successful writer without first being a reader.

Take Online Courses:

Enroll in online courses related to writing, content creation, SEO, or any other skill you want to develop. Platforms like Coursera, Skillshare, and Udemy offer a variety of courses taught by industry profession-als.

Take part in Writing Workshops:

Attend writing workshops or join writing groups in your local community or online. Constructive feed-back from peers and mentors can help you refine your writing style.

Attend Webinars and Seminars:

Participate in webinars and seminars hosted by in-dustry experts. These events often provide insights into the latest trends, tools, and techniques in the writing and content creation space.

Practice Regularly:

Writing, like any skill, improves with consistent practice. Set aside dedicated time each day or week for writing exercises, journaling, or working on per-sonal projects. While waiting for that first project, start writing an ebook focused on your niche. It might become a nice addition to your marketing arsenal.

Specialize in a Niche:

Choose a niche or industry to specialize in. Deep-ening your knowledge in a specific area not only makes you more attractive to clients in that industry, but also allows you to develop expertise.

Allow online news aggregator sites to send you updates in the fields that influence your niche.

Learn SEO Basics:

Understanding Search Engine Optimization (SEO) is valuable for online content creators. Learn the basics of SEO to optimize your content for search engines and increase its visibility.

Experiment with Different Formats:

Explore different writing formats, such as blog posts, articles, case studies, and whitepapers. Each format comes with its own set of challenges and requirements, helping you diversify your skill set.

Stay Informed:

Keep yourself updated on industry trends, writing tools, and technological advancements. Follow relevant blogs, subscribe to newsletters, and take part in online discussions to stay informed.

Seek Feedback:

Actively seek feedback on your writing. Join writing communities or share your work with mentors and peers who can provide constructive criticism.

Collaborate with Others:

Collaborate with other writers, designers, or professionals in related fields. Working on collaborative projects exposes you to different perspectives and skill sets.

Learn Graphic Design Basics:

Familiarize yourself with basic graphic design principles. Knowing how to create visually appealing content or work with graphic designers can enhance the overall quality of your projects.

Master Editing and Proofreading:

Develop strong editing and proofreading skills. Attention to detail is crucial in professional writing, and being able to edit your work effectively improves the quality of your output. Consider installing an app like ProWritingAid to assist you.

Stay Open to Feedback:

Be open to receiving feedback and constructive criticism. Use feedback as a tool for growth and improvement.

Network with Professionals.

Connect with professionals in your industry or niche. Networking can provide valuable insights, mentorship opportunities, and potential collaborations that contribute to your skill development.

Skill development is an ongoing process. Embrace a mindset of continuous learning and actively seek opportunities to enhance your abilities as a freelance writer.

Chapter 11

MARKET YOURSELF

Effectively marketing yourself as a new free-lance writer is essential for attracting clients and building a successful career. Here are some key strategies to market yourself:

1. **Create a Professional Website:**

   ○ Develop a professional website showcasing your portfolio, services, and contact information. A well-designed website provides a centralized platform for potential clients to learn about your skills and experience. If creating a website is beyond your comfort level, then explore sites like Fiverr to find someone who will build a website for you. Or ask one of your grandkids

2. **Optimize Your LinkedIn Profile:**

○ Create an interesting LinkedIn profile that highlights your expertise, skills, and writing samples. Connect with professionals in your industry and participate in relevant LinkedIn groups.

3. **Use Social Media:**

○ Establish a presence on social media platforms like X/Twitter, Facebook, and Instagram. Share your writing insights, industry news, and links to your work. Engage with your audience and build a community around your brand.

4. **Guest Blogging:**

○ Contribute guest posts to reputable blogs in your niche. Guest blogging not only exposes your writing to a wider audience, but also establishes you as an authority in your field.

5. **Network on Freelance Platforms:**

○ Join freelance platforms such as Upwork, Freelancer, or Fiverr. Create a professional profile, bid on relevant projects, and actively engage with potential clients.

6. **Offer Free Resources:**

○ Create valuable and shareable content that showcases your expertise. This could include blog posts, downloadable guides, a short ebook, cheat sheets, or infographics. Distribute these resources through your website and social media channels. Be sure there is a way for the reader to contact you.

7. **Build an Email List:**

○ Create an email newsletter to stay in touch with clients and prospects. Share updates, relevant content, and exclusive offers to keep your audience engaged.

8. **Ask for Referrals:**

○ Request referrals from satisfied clients. Word of mouth is a powerful marketing tool, and positive recommendations can significantly affect your freelance writing business.

9. Take Part in Online Communities:

- Join online forums, groups, or communities related to writing or your specific niche. Engage in discussions, answer questions, and share your expertise to establish yourself as a valuable contributor. Quora offers many different groups that may give you access to your niche. You will be able to ask and answer questions with other like-minded people.

10. Create a Blog:

- Start a blog on your website to showcase your writing style, share industry insights, and demonstrate your expertise. Regularly updating your blog can attract organic traffic and potential clients.

11. Collaborate with Other Freelancers:

- Collaborate with other freelancers or professionals in related fields. This can lead to cross-promotional opportunities and introduce your services to a broader audience.

12. **Attend Networking Events:**

- Attend virtual or in-person networking events, conferences, and workshops. These events provide valuable opportunities to connect with potential clients and other professionals in the writing industry.

13. **Offer Special Promotions:**

- Introduce special promotions or discounts for new clients. This can incentivize clients to try your services and establish an initial relationship.

14. **Showcase Testimonials:**

- Display client testimonials prominently on your website and marketing materials. Positive feedback builds trust and credibility with potential clients.

15. **Invest in Paid Advertising.**

- ○ Consider targeted paid advertising on platforms like Google Ads, LinkedIn, or social media. This can increase your visibility and reach potential clients who are actively seeking freelance writing services.

Remember, effective marketing is an ongoing effort. Consistency in your efforts and a focus on building relationships will contribute to the long-term success of your freelance writing business.

Chapter 12

ARTIFICIAL INTELLIGENCE or AI

So, the question is, can artificial intelligence help you as a freelance writer? The short answer is yes. The longer answer is yes, but you need to learn how to use it to help you. This boils down to creating the right "prompts" to enter into the search box and then refining until the information you need is useful.

At the time of writing this book, artificial intelligence is creating a firestorm of controversy. Tried, true and established authors, especially those of the fiction variety, seem to take the stance that AI is the devil incarnate. I'm not so sure. New technology has always been challenging on many levels. I recall as a young lad that using an electronic calculator to do math was a mortal sin. I may yet go to hell, especially if my grade 5 teacher, Sister Mary Joseph, knew that I now have one on the phone that I carry in my pocket!

There are some bad actors out there who are asking an AI app to create stories and then they upload them to various book selling sites and sell them as is. They are creating rubbish and attempting to get rich quick. Here is what I know about using AI as of this time: it has a very useful place to <u>assist</u> in research, outlining and defining concepts, especially difficult to understand things. The key to using it successfully is learning how to ask questions and keep asking them until you get a proper answer. When I was younger, we used to call this part of the world a library and Encyclopedia Britannica. Today, the repository of all information is the internet.

The art of wording inquiries, or prompts and then determining how to proceed from there is rapidly becoming a whole new industry and one you might want to learn about. This author recently viewed a question on an AI app that asked it to explain Quantum Physics in language that a 5 year old would understand. The information it created was amusing and I learned a lot. Potential clients for your freelance writing services may want you to generate documentation for them faster and more accurately – AI is probably the answer.

Some people, thanks to the media, have decided that it is a new and foreboding technology and insist on showing pictures of scary looking robots from horror movies in their presentations. Here are a few examples of artificial intelligence at work that you may already know: smart home devices like Alexa, Google Home and more, self-driving cars, Netflix and Spotify recommendations, auto complete in Google Search and messaging apps, Facebook and Instagram, Spell and Grammar check in Word. We have been using it for years.

A recommendation: if you decide to use apps like Chat/GPT and any of the many others, it is essential that you take into consideration any ethical and moral issues. Amazon is now requiring writers to acknowledge if AI was used and how it was used to create books. This author thinks we will come to accept the value and input of AI soon and look at it as a useful tool to increase productivity.

The internet and social media are swirling with articles on artificial intelligence including "how-to's" and warnings. Therefore, if you are thinking about accessing its help, it would be a good idea to keep up with current thought.

Chapter 13

Summary:

Freelance writing offers a flexible and rewarding career path for individuals with a passion for words. As a freelance writer, you have the freedom to choose your projects, set your own schedule, and work from virtually anywhere. Building a successful freelance writing business involves creating a professional online presence, networking, and continually expanding your skills. Whether you're a seasoned professional or just starting, there are various platforms, tools, and strategies to help you succeed in the freelance writing world.

If you have a way with words and a desire for independence, freelance writing could be your key to a fulfilling, part-time retirement career. Embrace the opportunities to showcase your creativity, specialize in niches you're passionate about, and connect with clients worldwide. With dedication, continuous learning, and effective self-promotion, you can turn your love for writing into a thriving opportunity. Take the plunge, explore the diverse world of freelance writing, and unlock the doors to a fun and flexible professional journey. Your words have power – let them pave the way to your freelance success!

Chapter 14

KEY TAKEAWAYS

Important Points about Freelance Writing:

Diverse Opportunities:

Freelance writing offers a vast array of opportunities, from content creation and blogging to copywriting and technical writing. Explore different niches to find where your passion and skills align.

Flexible Lifestyle:

Enjoy the flexibility of setting your own schedule and working from anywhere. Freelance writing allows you to balance work with personal life, accommodating various lifestyles and commitments.

Build a Strong Online Presence:

A professional online presence, including a well-crafted website and engaging social media profiles, is essential for attracting clients and showcasing your writing skills.

Continuous Learning:

Stay committed to continuous learning. Regularly expand your writing skills, stay updated on industry trends, and embrace new tools and technologies to remain competitive.

Networking Matters:

Actively participate in online and offline communities, attend events, and build relationships with other freelancers, clients, and professionals in your niche. Networking can open doors to new opportunities.

Clear Communication:

Effective communication is key. Clearly articulate your skills, experience, and the value you bring to clients. Tailor your proposals and messages to each client's needs.

Set Realistic Rates:

Determine your rates based on industry standards, your skills, and the value you provide. Start with competitive rates, and adjust them as you gain experience and expertise.

Create a Portfolio:

Build a comprehensive portfolio showcasing your best work. Include a variety of samples that highlight your versatility and expertise in different writing styles and formats.

Embrace Specialization:

Consider specializing in a niche or industry. Specialization enhances your credibility and can lead to higher-paying opportunities within a specific market.

Client Relationships Matter:

Foster positive relationships with clients. Deliver high-quality work on time, communicate effectively, and seek feedback to improve your services.

Promote Yourself:

Actively market yourself through various channels, including freelance platforms, social media, and your own website. Share valuable content, engage with your audience, and consistently promote your services.

Adaptability is Key:

Stay adaptable to industry changes, client needs, and emerging trends. The ability to adapt ensures your continued success in the dynamic world of freelance writing.

Balancing Creativity and Professionalism:

Find the balance between creativity and professionalism. While creativity is essential for engaging content, maintaining a professional image is crucial for attracting and retaining clients.

Time Management:

Develop strong time management skills to meet deadlines and handle multiple projects efficiently. Prioritize tasks, set realistic goals, and maintain a healthy work-life balance.

Persistence Pays Off.

Building a successful freelance writing career takes time and persistence. Stay dedicated to honing your craft, expanding your network, and adapting to the ever-evolving landscape of freelance writing.

Afterword

And so, my retiring friend, as we draw the curtains on this delightful exploration of freelance writing, let's recap the magical perks awaiting you in this world of wordsmithery.

Picture this: A life where your creativity knows no bounds, your schedule dances to your own tune, and the only boss you answer to is that quirky, invisible character who lives in your writing corner (yes, the one who insists on using semicolons in every sentence).

Freelance writing isn't just about crafting sentences; it's about crafting a lifestyle where every click of a key adds a brushstroke to the canvas of your retirement adventure. The flexibility, the diverse opportunities, and the joy of turning your passion into profit—it's a retirement dream come true.

So, why not swap the rocking chair for a writing desk? Dive into the world of freelance writing, where every day is a new chapter waiting to be written, and your retirement becomes a tapestry of stories, creativity, and fun. Cheers to a new chapter and the boundless possibilities of freelance writing!

"I'm retired and don't want any additional income..." said no one ever!

If you have found value in **THE PROSPEROUS PEN**, we would appreciate you leaving a review on the site where you bought it. Here is a brief review of the books in the **EXTRA RETIREMENT INCOME IS SEXY** series.

This series of books, **EXTRA RETIREMENT INCOME IS SEXY**, includes many, many possibilities for retirees to add more income and enjoy more creative pursuits. Here is a brief review of the other books:

Freelance Writing: Many websites and businesses constantly need content. If you enjoy writing, you could offer your services as a freelance writer. There are platforms like Upwork and Fiverr that connect writers with clients. We will explore this opportunity in depth in book 2, **THE PROSPEROUS PEN**.

Online Tutoring: If you have expertise in a particular subject, you could offer online tutoring services. Platforms like Chegg Tutors or Wyzant allow you to connect with students seeking help. More information about online tutoring is available in book 3 of this series, **DIGITAL CLASSROOMS**.

Virtual Assistance: Many entrepreneurs and small businesses need help with tasks like email management, data entry, and scheduling. Offering virtual assistance services can be a great way to use your organizational skills. We will dive into becoming a virtual assistant in book 4, **SILVER HAIRED SAGE**.

Sell Handmade Crafts or Digital Items: If you have a talent for crafting or have accumulated unique vintage items, you can sell them on platforms like Etsy or eBay. Creating digital products like ebooks, courses and journals can lead to a world of opportunity. This exciting area of income generation is fully explained in book 5, **DESIGNING WEALTH.**

Take part in Online Surveys and Reviews: While this may not generate a substantial income, participating in online surveys can provide a small stream of income. Websites like Swagbucks or Survey Junkie offer opportunities to earn money for your opinions. Creating and sharing product reviews can lead to a very substantial income generating business.

We offer all the details of this business idea in book 6, ***GOLDEN INSIGHTS***.

About the Author

Robert J Bannon is still trying to define what retirement is and how to live it. Leveraging his life as an entrepreneur, sales manager, stockbroker and VP investor relations, along with 10 years as a tax consultant, Bob has written a 6 book series, EXTRA RETIREMENT INCOME IS SEXY, to help retirees create additional income and fulfillment in their life. He has also authored several other non-fiction titles, some of which are included below.

He and his wife live in the foothills of the Rockies and have 2 adult children and 3 grandsons. He continues to travel the world, play golf, and write, balanced with grocery shopping, cooking, and afternoon naps. You can reach him through his website at RobertJBannon.com.

amazon.com/

Also By Robert J Bannon

EXTRA RETIREMENT INCOME IS SEXY
Ignite Your Financial Passion and Live the
Lifestyle You Love
BOOK 1
Paperback ISBN 978-0-9739646-9-1
Ebook ISBN 978-1-7382603-0-0

THE PROSPEROUS PEN
Mastering Freelance Writing for Retirement
Riches
Book 2
Paperback ISBN 978-1-7382603-1-7
Ebook ISBN 978-1-7382603-2-4

DIGITAL CLASSROOMS

Unlocking Retirement Riches as an Online Tutor

Book 3

Paperback ISBN 978-1-7382603-3-1

Ebook ISBN 978-1-7382603-4-8

SILVER HAIRED SAGE

Retirees Become Amazing Virtual Assistants & Increase Their Own Income

Book 4

Paperback ISBN 978-1-7382603-5-5

Ebook ISBN 978-1-7382603-6-2

DESIGNING WEALTH

A Retiree's Guide to More Income and Creative Fulfillment

Book 5

Paperback ISBN 978-1-7382603-7-9

Ebook ISBN 978-1-7382603-8-6

GOLDEN INSIGHTS

Unlocking Extra Income – A Retiree's Guide to Surveys & Reviews

Book 6

Paperback ISBN 978-1-7382603-9-3

Ebook ISBN   978-1-7382622-0-5

EASY STOCK MARKET STARTER COURSE
ASIN B09NCFC2FF   ISBN 979-8783059315

THE WEST COAST TRAIL: One Step at a Time
ASIN 172789703X   ISBN 978-1727897036

THE ONE HOUR AUTHOR: Non-Fiction Book Writing for Busy People
ASIN 1470135493   ISBN 978-1470135492

By Lonewolf Notes/RJB
ETSY SHOP MANAGER
ASIN B083XW6CXJ   ISBN 979-8601305228

MY WINE TASTING JOURNAL & NOTEBOOK
ASIN 1676781633   ISBN 978-1676781639

FINANCIAL PLANNER TEMPLATE
ASIN 1676048227   ISBN 978-1676048220

www.ingramcontent.com/pod-product-compliance
Lightning Source LLC
Chambersburg PA
CBHW070943210326
41520CB00021B/7026